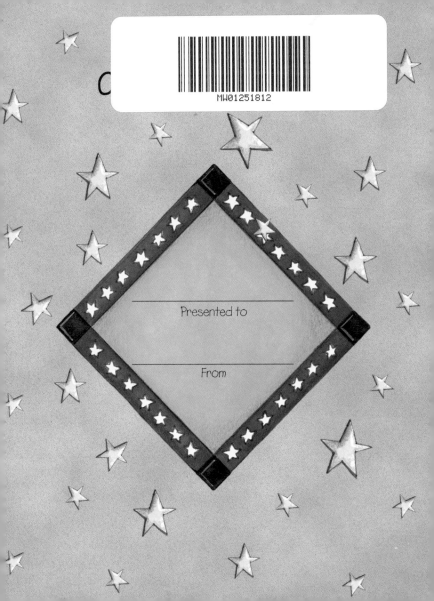

Presented to

_____

From

A graduate
is someone
to celebrate!

I Celebrate You,™ Graduate!

Illustrated by Beverly Burge

To grow
smarter
and kinder—
that is
real success.

What matters
is what you do
with what
you've got.

Here are some of
the wonderful traits
that make you special—

If you think
you can,
you can.
If you want to,
you will.

Go for
the great!

I'm proud of you!

If I could pick and choose
any gift in the world for you,
I'd give you the best
for a life of success...

I'd give you the gift of

_____

_____

Award

presented to you for

Certificate
of
Merit

SCRAPBOOK

Sing your own song... the one from your heart.

Destiny is
a thing to
be achieved.

I'm **DELIGHTED**
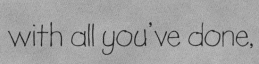
with all you've done,
ENCOURAGED
by your efforts,
and **PROUD** of your
PERSEVERANCE!

I have great confidence in you!

Your life
is an
awesome
gift from
God.

Keep an open **HEART**—
for loving,
an open **MIND**—
for learning,
and open **HANDS**—
for giving.

You are on your way to becoming all that God wants you to be!

This is my prayer
for you graduate—

_____

_____

_____

_____

_____

_____

_____

_____

_____

FULFILL your dreams,
FOLLOW your heart.
MAKE choices that
will lead you where
you want to go.